CW01083330

JAPANESE TREASURE TALES.

Japanese Treasure Tales

THE AMA AND THE JEWEL.

(From a Sword Guard in
Mr. G. Ambrose Lee's collection.)

JAPANESE
TREASURE TALES.

BY

KUMASAKU TOMITA

AND

G. AMBROSE LEE.

(With Thirty seven illustrations).

"The many coloured tablets bright
With loves and wars of old."
Macaulay

YAMANAKA & Co.,

LONDON:
68, NEW BOND STREET,
W.

JAPAN.
MAIN HOUSE, OSAKA.
Branch House
AWATA, KIOTO.

TO

MRS HUGH FRASER,

WHO,

BY HER WRITINGS,

HAS DONE MUCH

TO DISSEMINATE IN ENGLAND

A KNOWLEDGE OF JAPAN.

CONTENTS.

ILLUSTRATIONS.

ILLUSTRATIONS.

INTRODUCTION.

Ever since I first came to England some six or seven years ago, I have had many enquiries for explanations of the incidents which occur so frequently in the art treasures of Japan, and also as to any English work in which the stories thus illustrated may be found. Such a book I have unfortunately not been able to name, the majority of English books on Japan being devoted to fairy tales, history or reviews of Japanese matters and general accounts of Japanese travels. I then formed the intention of endeavouring myself to produce such a book, and on consulting my colleague, Mr. Lee, he not only cordially approved of my design but offered to assist me in every way possible towards its execution, and the present little volume is the result. In its preparation many unlooked for difficulties arose, such as, a scarcity of original Japanese authorities on some of the subjects, a difficulty in finding suitable treasures with which to illustrate some of the stories, and others which it is needless to specify. The tales, such as they are, are all constructed from the best available Japanese authorities, in most cases much of the original which is of the nature of mere padding is omitted, and, in conclusion, the little work is not intended for the serious study of historians or philosophers, but is merely a humble contribution towards a knowledge of Japanese art, such as may, it is hoped, appeal to admirers of the same.

We wish to acknowledge with sincere thanks the courtesy of those who, for the purposes of illustration, have placed their collections at our disposal, and whose names will be found beneath each object illustrated; and thanks are returned also to Messrs. Yamanaka and Kado, who have helped us in our work

KUMASAKU TOMITA

3rd January, 1906

(For the information of those who do not happen to have had the subject brought to their attention, a Tsuba is the guard of a sword, through which the blade passes. It is usually made of a flat piece of iron or other metal, and is frequently decorated. A Netsuke may be described as a toggle to which the cords supporting the medicine case (Inrō), tobacco pouch or pouch, are attached, and which is tucked into the girdle, from which the latter depend. Netsukes are made of wood, ivory, horn, pottery and a variety of other materials, and are usually carved to represent some figure or group of figures, flower, bird, beast or natural object).

I.

ROCHISHIN.

(China, 12th Century A.D.)

ROCHISHIN began his career as a sort of detective attached to the primitive police service of Ishū, his native place. One day, a pretty little singing girl, attached to a restaurant in the place, appealed to him to protect her against a burly butcher, who had a shop close by, and who alleged that he possessed a paper—which the little singer asserted was a forgery—in which she promised either to repay to the butcher a large sum of money, said to have been borrowed by her, or to become his slave, a fate to which she had the very strongest objection. Rochishin, touched by her entreaties, bade her cheer up, promising to go round and just talk matters over with the butcher in question, whose name was Tei. The little confabulation which ensued was scarcely, from the butcher's point of view, a success, for Rochishin unfortunately happened to lose his temper, and knock the butcher over, and the latter shewing no disposition to get up again, proved on examination to be unquestionably defunct. Now, as the chronicler tersely remarks, even in China—where these events took place—murder was not permitted, especially to a detective officer, so Rochishin thought it prudent to lose no time in quietly evacuating his post, and on confiding the circumstances of the case to his friend Choingai, the latter persuaded him that his best chance of safety lay in becoming a monk; so, though not a particularly promising novice, Rochishin sought for and obtained admittance to the great monastery of Manjūin in Gotaisan.

Now the first "prohibitions" or laws of a Buddhist monastery are:—Not to kill any living creature, whatsoever; not to steal or covet anything; never to drink intoxicating drink; to strictly observe celibacy and never to tell lies, and Rochishin very promptly arrived at the conclusion that he had no vocation for keeping such an uncomfortably comprehensive rule, and made it therefore his immediate business to break it on every convenient occasion. The good monks had no use for such an unruly companion, and with little delay he was solemnly expelled by the abbot of the monastery. Rochishin, considerably relieved, departed, and going to a smith, directed him to make a sort of iron club, five feet long, and weighing sixty-two pounds, which he named "Kaijo," or "the warning stick." Armed with this pretty little weapon, he struck up an alliance with Yoshi, a well-known robber, who was the head of a gang of robbers who infested the district, and the two, with their party, broke into the Honjūji temple, which had been taken possession of by a rival gang of robbers, whom they dispersed and whose leader Rochishin killed with his club. The latter, after this exploit, became the head of Yoshi's party

Some years after these events, Rochishin joined his set of robbers with those led by a celebrated freebooter named Soko, in Riosanpaku, and became celebrated all over China as "Hana Osho," or the "flower monk," from the pattern of flowers tatooed all over his body. The evil of these marauding bands at length grew to such an extent that all the available troops of the Government were sent against them, but in five battles the robbers were successful, and the Emperor at last, in despair, made terms with them and in the third year of Senwa (circa A.D. 1120) pardoned them all, and hoped they wouldn't do it again. Rochishin himself set out for Kyōto, and on his way there he stayed at the Rokuwaji temple, where he was found one day at ebb-tide *dead, in a flower-scented room, in the attitude of prayer. His rather questionable exploits appealed to the popular sense of right and honour, and in Japan he holds a place somewhat analogous to the English Robin Hood.

II.

TADAMORI AND THE OIL THIEF.

(Japan, 1178 A.D.)

Tadamori was a junior officer in the Imperial Guards, and it was his duty at one time to accompany the retired emperor Shira

* In both China and Japan it is believed that natural death always takes place when the tide is ebbing, and birth when it is flowing

THE LADY YOKIHI.

(From an Ivory Netsuke, Mr. W. L. Behrens's collection.)

ROCHISHIN.

(From an Inlaid Iron Sword Guard in Mr G. A. Lee's collection.)

Kawa-Hono on his frequent visits to his lady love, the beautiful Gion Niogio, who lived at the far side of the Gion temple in Kyōto. On leaving home in the early evening of a rainy day in May (May in Japan is the rainy season) they came to a grove on the south side of the Gion temple, where they caught sight of a curious shining monster flitting about amongst the trees, appearing and disappearing in different directions. The apparition seemed to have a scarlet face and a great mop of bristling hair, like silver wire, while in its hand it carried a mallet. Alarmed at this sinister vision, the emperor sent Tadamori forward to inspect it, who with desperate courage pounced on the monster and without any difficulty secured it. It proved to be quite mortal and harmless, being neither more nor less than a servant monk or laybrother of the temple, going his rounds to replenish the oil in the lanterns in the temple gardens. On his head was a bundle of barley straw to keep off the rain, while in one hand he carried the oil-can and in the other the little hand light, whose rays lit up the wet straw and his face, in such a way as to produce the eerie effect which had so alarmed the emperor.

(Another version of the story makes the intruder someone who had come in to the gardens to steal the oil from the temple lanterns, and the story is thus sometimes known as that of "The Oil Thief.")

III.

"KIKUJIDO" OR "THE CHRYSANTHEMUM BOY."

KING BOKUO, who reigned for fifty-five years in China, 8th century, B.C., had a favourite page named Jido. On one occasion when in attendance on the King, the boy accidentally kicked a pillow of his master's bed. According to the rigid etiquette of ancient Chinese court circles this was really a most heinous offence, and its commission involved the culprit in unknown but terrible penalties, and the King therefore, who sincerely liked the lad, endeavoured to hush the matter up and keep it secret But all in vain; for, in spite of the royal solicitude the occurrence leaked out and became common property. The details of the case came at length before

TOFŪ AND THE FROG.

(From an Ivory Netsuke, Mr. H. S. Trower's collection.)

TADAMORI AND THE OIL THIEF.

(From a Wooden Netsuke in Mr. W. L. Behrens's collection.)

the high officials of the court, entrusted with the onerous task of dealing judicially with such serious matters, and then, in due course, all possible extenuating circumstances having been taken into consideration, the convicted culprit was sentenced as an "offender against the majesty of the King" to perpetual banishment on a mountain three hundred ri distant from the king's palace. The King was deeply grieved at this decision, but even his authority was not sufficient to override the rigid laws of the court and nation, and off Jido went to his exile. But before he departed the King gave him a secret audience, at which he presented the exile with two Buddhist verses, the recital of which would blot out all his sins and ensure his eternal salvation. Jido was then led off and imprisoned far inside the mountainous valley of Tetken, where he occupied himself in continually reciting the stanzas in question, which proved a charm of power to keep all noxious creatures and all illness from him. Fearing that in spite of his devotion he might forget the stanzas, Jido took the precaution of writing them on the leaves of a chrysanthemum plant, and their efficacy was such that the dew of the plant became as sweet as honey, and those who drank of it never felt hunger In prayer and contemplation Jido's life passed tranquilly by, he being happier far than when he was at court. He lived to a great age but preserved much of his youthful appearance even to the end.

IV.

ONO TOFU AND THE FROG.

(Japan, 928 A.D.)

In both China and Japan, penmanship or writing is considered an art in itself, on a par with drawing and painting, or even perhaps above the latter arts, since writing is an absolutely necessary accomplishment in social life, whilst drawing and painting are rather of the nature of luxuries.

Tōfū, the subject of our little story, was a man of birth and position in Japan, but his writing was very shockingly bad, and he reached the age of sixty years before it had emerged from, as it were, the pothooks and hangers of childhood. He had, however, the grace to be thoroughly ashamed of it. One day in spring, after a shower, he went out for a walk in a suburb of Kyōto, and, coming to a place in the road where a willow tree grew, one of the branches of which hung down to within a short distance of the ground, his attention was attracted by a frog which was endeavouring to jump from the ground on to this pendant branch. By jumping vigorously the frog could just touch the branch, but being unable to obtain a foothold necessarily fell down each time it tried. Again and again the attempt was made, in vain; until, exhausted with its efforts, the panting frog appeared to give up the struggle, and indeed Tōfū watching concluded that it had done so. But after resting for a time, the frog again began jumping in a still more determined manner, and after countless failures at length secured a foothold and made its way up the tree as if proud of its success. Tōfū was much impressed by the frog's exploit, and regarding the encounter as a lesson for himself, determined to make equally resolute efforts to learn to write properly In this determination, like the frog, he so persevered that after a few years he not only acquired proficiency, but became very famous as the best writer in Japan. Later in life, when he was quite an old man, the Emperor Daigo Tenno commissioned him to write the names on a series of portraits of sages and heroes, which had been painted by a very skilful artist, Kose Kanaoka, on the shoji of the Shishin-den or Throne Room of the palace.

The Japanese consider that our hero, Sangi Sari, and Dainagon Gyozei, who both lived after him, are the three greatest experts in caligraphy known to history.

V.

SHOKI AND THE DEMON.

(China, 8th Century A.D.)

THE Emperor Gensokotei (who reigned in China from 714 to 755 A.D.) was one night, in a dream, furiously attacked by a terrible demon, but just as the monarch was about to succumb, a gigantic figure, armed, and of the most resolute aspect, made its appearance, and quickly put the demon to death "Who are you," cried the Emperor to his deliverer, "and why have you rescued me thus?" The gigantic apparition made a profound obeisance and replied, "My name is Shoki, once of Shunanzan. In my lifetime I twice failed to qualify myself for the highest official rank to which I aspired Shame and despair so possessed me that I committed suicide, by knocking my head against a stone pillar. Your imperial ancestor, the Emperor Koso, who reigned a hundred years ago, touched with compassion, assigned to me at my death the honours which I, alas, had been unable to secure in my life, and directed that my body should be attired in the state robes, and that my funeral should be conducted with the ceremonial and escort due to a Minister of State. For these consoling attentions I am most profoundly grateful, and my spirit lives always to guard and protect the descendants of my kind benefactor." With these words the apparition vanished. On awaking soon afterwards, the Emperor with the vision still clearly in his mind, sent for a celebrated painter named Godoshi, whom he commissioned to execute a portrait of his visionary champion, from the description which he gave him of it, and thus Shoki, "the Demon Queller," became one of the most popular figures in the art of China and Japan.

VI.

ROSEI.

THERE once lived, near Shoku in China, a man named Rosei, whose great ambition was to acquire great riches; but in spite of all his efforts he was quite unable to raise himself from his original state of penury. Hearing that a great sage was residing at Yohizan, which was some days' journey from his home, Rosei made up his mind to pay this learned person a visit, with a view of asking him how to get riches. On his journey he had to pass through the town of Kantan where, as night was approaching, he decided to stay until morning. Entering an inn, he ordered supper, and while he was waiting for the millet—of which it consisted—to be cooked, the inn-keeper offered him the use of a pillow,

SHOKI AND THE DEMON.
(From an old Ivory Netsuke in Mr. Walter L. Behrens's collection.)

TENAGA AND ASHINAGA.
(From an Ivory Netsuke in Mr. O. C. Raphael's collection.)

which, he jokingly said, would tell him all he desired to know. Rosei being tired with his journey gratefully accepted the offer and lay down to rest, but had scarcely done so, when he was roused by a messenger who came to the inn to ask for him, saying, "I want to have speech with Rosei who is here." "Who are you?" Rosei asked. "I am come to tell you that you have been elected King of Sō, and that the ceremony of your coronation awaits but your presence," replied the messenger. "Me?" said Rosei, "Impossible! There must be some mistake. I have no right whatever to the office you speak of." "There is indeed no mistake, sir," the messenger replied, "you have the good fortune to reign over this country, so be pleased to take your seat in this kago." Rosei did so, and was immediately borne away to a splendid palace, in which he was installed and crowned. The palace consisted of a series of great buildings, capped with clouds. The paths of the surrounding gardens were formed of pale silver-like and dark gold-like sands, with gates of polished jade, and through them passed beautifully dressed courtiers and ladies, decked with every description of precious gems, and many other folk bringing an endless tribute of splendid treasures and curious works of art. Thousands of gaily embroidered flags fluttered on the roofs of the palace On the east of the palace the golden rays of the sun shone on a hill three hundred feet high, looking like silver, while on the west was another mountain looking like gold under the silvery light of the full moon.

Here Rosei reigned in unexampled splendour for many years, until one day a great Minister of State told him that if he drank some saké out of a certain precious cup—called Kogainohai—he would live for a thousand years. Rosei immediately determined to take this wonderful elixir, and a great feast was prepared, at which a magnificent company of court ladies and nobles assembled. The feast proceeded with song and dance, the wine appeared inexhaustible. Over the palace the moon rose in tranquil beauty, to later on give place to the glorious dawn and this to the effulgence of noonday; this again to the twilight and the soft night breezes. And still the feast went on. In the gardens it seemed as if the flowers of spring mingled with the leaves of autumn, the tender blush of the cherry blossom with the vivid crimson and orange of the dying maples: while at the same time on the delicate branches appeared the soft paddings of the snows of mid-winter, and the wind blew through the thousand trees and the luxuriant grasses of autumn: all the four seasons, as it were, grouped together round the palace walls:—

"The millet is cooked, your dinner is quite ready," said the innkeeper, as Rosei stretched himself, opened his eyes, and looked round. All the splendour was vanished. The beautiful ladies who danced and sang so sweetly were replaced by the wind sighing through the swaying branches of the pine trees, the palace by the rough little Kantan inn, and the luxurious life of fifty years resolved itself into the time consumed in cooking millet. "God be praised," said Rosei, "even the apparently exhaustless pleasures of hundreds of years of life would appear nothing but a dream when the end of life shall come. Well, this pillow is sage enough for me, for it has given me indeed an answer to the question I would have asked." And homeward he turned.

VII.

SHIRO AND THE BOAR.

(Japan, 12th Century A.D.)

YORITOMO—the founder of the Shogunate, and himself the first Shogun—settled in Kamakura near Yedo, in 1192 A.D. In the following May, he invited all the great Daimios to meet him on a certain day at the base of Fujiyama, for a great hunting expedition. In obedience to this invitation a great party—popularly said to number ten thousand (the Japanese are very fond of numbers, especially thousands) Daimios and their suites assembled for the purpose under innumerable tents—a unique assembly in the history of Japan. On the third day of the hunt, a wild boar, of unusual size and ferocity, although already wounded by four or five arrow shots, dashed towards the Shogun, who, seeing his danger, called to a brave samurai named Shiro Nitta, who was waiting by, to kill the infuriated beast. Without a moment's hesitation, Shiro, as the boar rushed past him, jumped straight from his horse on to the boar's back, holding on with one hand to the creature's tail as if it were a bridle, while with the other he drew his wakizashi (shorter of the two swords worn by gentlemen) and stabbed the boar deeply five or six times. With a piteous moan the poor beast expired, not falling however, since by the impetus of its desperate flight, its legs remained stuck firmly some four or five inches in the soft ground. Yoritomo, conceiving that he owed his life to Shiro's bravery and resource, as a recognition thereof, endowed him with an estate of five hundred cho.*

VIII.

KOUFU AND THE SAKE SHOP.

(China.)

A POOR man named Koufū once lived in China and was, in spite of his poverty, of a mild and pious disposition. One night he dreamt that he would become rich if he started selling saké in the town of Yoshi. With

* About 150 acres.

some difficulty he succeeded in doing so, and as predicted, his enterprise was successful and he became quite well-to-do. For a long time he was visited every day by a strange customer, who remained many hours steadily drinking bottles of saké, but never apparently getting drunk. At length, unable to contain his curiosity regarding his mysterious customer any longer, one day Koufū asked him his name. "I am Shojo and live in the sea," was the reply, as the weird personage glided away, never to return. From which incident the representation of Shojo is regarded as a luck bringer to the faithful user thereof.

IX.

THE LADY YOKIHI.

(China, 8th Century B.C.)

THE Emperor Gensokotei, who reigned in China in the eighth century, came to the throne at a period of universal peace: the happy result of his predecessor's wisdom and courage. But no sooner was he securely settled than he abandoned himself to a career

ROSEI.

(*From a Sword Guard in*
Mr. H. Seymour Trower's collection.)

of folly and dissipation. In his various palaces he collected a vast number—some say three thousand—of beautiful ladies, in no ways remarkable for the strictness of their manners or morals. Amongst these venal beauties was one named Yōkihi who was not only exceedingly lovely but was moreover most kindhearted, brilliant and cultivated. With her the Emperor became entirely infatuated, neglecting even those few duties which he had hitherto performed, to devote himself entirely to her Her father was made Prime Minister, and her other relatives placed in the highest official positions; which unfortunate favouritism resulted promptly in a serious rebellion, in which the government troops were entirely overthrown by the rebels, and the Emperor and Yōkihi compelled to fly to the mountains, with the remains of his armies. On their way thither some of the officers, attributing all their misfortunes to the Emperor, and his to the evil influence of Yōkihi, set upon and put the lady to death. The poor Emperor was inconsolable at his loss, and his mind even became unhinged, until many months afterwards, a Sennin called on him, stating that he knew how keenly the

Emperor felt the loss of Yōkihi, with whom the Sennin could communicate, if the Emperor desired it, and endeavour to obtain from her some communication for her lover. The Emperor eagerly assented, whereupon the Sennin, enveloped in a cloud, disappeared. In a splendid cloudlike palace he found Yōkihi, who told him that she was continually aware of the state of the Emperor's feelings towards her, which on her part she entirely reciprocated, but that her life was now so different to his that she could not directly communicate with him. She however gave the Sennin, with a loving message, a gold kanzashi (hair pin) to present to the Emperor on his return. On receipt of this communication, the infatuated Emperor killed himself, in the expectation of meeting his lost love in another life.

X.

SABURO AND THE FISHERMAN.

(Japan, 12th Century A D.)

Sasaki Saburo Moritsuma was one of the generals under the command of Yoritomo's (the first Shogun's) brother Noriyori, during the campaign in 1184 A.D., when the Heishi family were being pursued from Kyōto to the west. The pursuing force, consisting of 30,000 officers and men, arrived one day at Kojima in the province of Bizen, where there was a ferry across an arm of the sea, on the opposite side of which, 25 cho (about two miles) across, the Heishi army was encamped. As the latter had naturally taken the precaution, after they crossed, of collecting every available boat, the Genji army was efficiently checked in its pursuit, and some days elapsed without any step being taken to continue it: though meanwhile some of the most intrepid spirits amongst the opposing forces came over in boats and shouted out taunts and challenges inviting their opponents to come over and fight. The baffled Genji were exceedingly furious, but could find no way of crossing the waters to reach the insolent enemy, until one night Saburo called on an old fisherman in the neighbourhood, and asked him if there was not any place sufficiently shallow for a man to ride across in safety on horseback. The fisherman replied that he knew of such a place at some distance off, which however changed with the changing moon; in the first half of the month it was towards the east, in the latter half towards the west of a certain spot, to which he offered to guide Saburo. On arriving at the place indicated by the fisherman, Saburo found that about three quarters of a mile was quite shallow water, while for the rest of the way the passage varied in depth from about the hip to the neck of a man, and was therefore perfectly passable by horsemen. Saburo thanked the fisherman, but distrusting the ability of "low class people" to keep a secret, and fearing that the secret of the ford might leak out, he suddenly decided to put it out of the power of the poor fisherman to disclose it to another, by there and then putting him to death.

On the following day Saburo led the whole army across the ford and, unmolested by the enemy, effected a landing on the opposite shore, continued the pursuit and eventually overcame his flying opponents.

When peace was concluded, the Shogun gave the place where the crossing occurred, to Saburo, praising him and declaring that though many rivers had been crossed on horseback, this was the first time that an army had thus crossed the sea. Saburo sought out the family of his fisherman guide, liberally provided for them, and moreover erected a monument to the memory of the man whom he had slain.

XI.

A KAMAKURA JUDGE.

(Japan, 17th Century.)

In feudal times, before the revolution, it was no uncommon thing for judges to accept bribes, or to yield to official pressure from high quarters in deciding cases which came before them. But Fujitsuna, a judge of Kamakura, was ever opposed to such practices, strictly doing his duty without fear or favour. In all matters which related to himself personally he was of a most economical turn of mind, and would have appeared mean and stingy, but that in charity, and indeed for every public and national purpose, he spent money cheerfully and even recklessly, never counting the cost if good were to be done. Once while passing over one of the Name-Kawa bridges he accidentally dropped ten mon of copper—i.e., about twopence half-penny—into the river. The judge immediately decided that this sum was not to be lost, and promptly engaged, at five mon apiece, ten men with torches, to search the river and recover the coins, which at length they succeeded in doing. A friend of Fujitsuna on hearing of the incident remarked to him that it did not pay to expend *fifty* mon in recovering *ten*, but Fujitsuna promptly replied, "You cannot have a very kind heart for the poor people whom I employed, or you would surely recognise what is waste of money and what is not. I lost, it is true, only ten mon, and if I had not at once recovered it, it would have been lost for good. But I paid fifty mon for torches to recover the ten, and therefore put into circulation altogether sixty mon which is thus available as part of the national assets." To which argument his friend had no reply.

XII. *

TENAGA ("Te"—Arm: "Naga"—Long) AND ASHINAGA ("Ashi"—Leg: "Naga"—Long).

In the book Sansaizuye, it is recorded that on the east of the Shakusui river is situated the long leg province, Ashinaga, close by the long arm province, Tenaga. The long-legged folks carried the long-armed people on their backs into the deep waters where the fish only could be caught. Neither could fish alone, for the long-armed man, having short legs, could not wade into the deep water, while the long-legged man although *he* could do so, could not catch fish when he got there, owing to his short arms Tradition asserts that the average length of arm of these people was nine feet, and that a pair of sleeves over ten feet long had been once picked up out of the sea, while the legs of the long-legged folk ran to fifteen feet.

---

* This is a common subject in the art of the country, chiefly in netsuke and kodzuka; sometimes the two figures are represented as engaged in a violent quarrel.

XIII.

TSUNA AND THE BEAUTIFUL LADY.

(Japan, 10th Century A.D.)

IN the winter of the year 974 A.D. the imperial city of Kyōto was much disturbed by some inexplicable occurrences, which caused considerable alarm to the inhabitants, and not without sufficient cause. For, a respectable citizen, while engaged with a group of friends would suddenly disappear, without his companions knowing how he was lost or ever seeing him again. At length these mysterious disappearances became so frequent that the matter spread through to the court circles, and the inhabitants of Kyōto all became infected with a sort of panic. All doors were closed before sunset, no one leaving his house after that time. In dread for the safety of the palace itself, as well as for the well-being of the good citizens, an order was at length issued to the bravest chiefs who were on guard in the several provinces—from Yedo to Kiushu—to at once proceed to Kyōto. Amongst these was Raiko, the governor of Shimosa, who came accompanied by his four brave attendants—amongst whom was Watanabe Tsuna, the hero of many a stirring tale of Japan—in the early part of April.

On the night of their arrival Raiko sent Tsuna out on an errand. On his return, by Ichijo Modoribashi Bridge, Tsuna met a beautiful girl, elegantly dressed, with a scarlet uchikise (head cover), her complexion of dazzling whiteness and her whole person perfumed with musk; she had also a kiyoh (Buddhist bible or scriptures) under her arm. As Tsuna came up to her, the maiden, with an air of perfect self-possession and dignity, addressed him saying, "Sir, will you have the kindness to direct me to my home at Gojō, it has become late and dark unexpectedly, and I am afraid." Tsuna, thinking however that if this were someone disguised, he would be on his guard, as he was suspicious of so young and beautiful a girl—and apparently a lady too—being out walking, unattended, so late at night, replied that he would escort her with much pleasure, and alighting from his horse, helped her to mount, himself leading the horse, while he walked beside. After going some distance towards Gojō, the girl told Tsuna that her home was not really there, but was outside Kyōto, and suggested that he should send her to it. Tsuna assented with "Yes, certainly," whereupon the appearance of the girl underwent a terrible change, and in her place he saw a fearful faced devil who roared out, "Well, my home is in Atagoyama mountain," and, seizing Tsuna by his top-knot of hair, flew off with him towards the mountains on the north-west of the city. Tsuna—who was not without experience in these matters—succeeded in drawing his sword, and with one skilful cut severed the arm, the hand of which grasped his head. With a howl of pain and rage, the demon sped away towards Atagoyama, while Tsuna fell down, alighting uninjured on the roof of the Kitano Temple. As soon as possible he detached the demon's hand from his hair, and found that instead of the snow-white skin of the lady of the bridge, it was all black covered with thick, white, stiff hairs. By a ruse the demon subsequently recovered its amputated limb, and presumably was able to get it neatly restored.

XIV.

CHOUN AND ATO.

(China, 3rd Century A D)

SOMEWHERE about the beginning of the third century A.D., the Chinese Emperor Gentoku took up his abode in the little castle of Shinya, and here he was besieged by his rival and enemy Soso, who brought a large army, and compelled Gentoku to abandon the defence and retreat towards the castle of Kako, hampered as he was by a host of his subjects, to whom his just and kindly rule had greatly endeared him, and who feared the tender mercies of his successful rival too much to remain and experience them. Soso after taking possession of Shinya, continued the pursuit of Gentoku's host, which, owing to the presence of so many non-combatants, was unable to move at all quickly and was soon overtaken. The rear-guard fought very desperately, but from the disparity in numbers was unable to check the victorious enemy. With the rear-guard Gentoku's own wife and son Ato were travelling, and during the latter part of the fighting were separated from the main part of the retreating host. When Chōun, the general in command of the rear-guard, became aware of this, he told himself that he could never meet his master Gentoku after having lost the latter's wife and child. He therefore gave up his command to a lieutenant, and tightening the strings of his helmet, turned his horse's head and dashed into the ranks of the pursuing enemy: in his desperate valour killing all who opposed him, but seeing no trace of the Empress and her son. At last, as he freed himself from the enemy's soldiers, who were continuing the pursuit, he met a friendly farmer, who, recognising him, told him where the lady was concealed, whom he presently found dying from a mortal wound, the child however being unharmed. The Empress expressed her satisfaction at seeing Chōun, and giving Ato to him, charged him to save the boy and deliver him to his father, the Emperor. Choun readily undertook to do so, or to die in the attempt, and mounting his horse he took the child up with him, and respectfully urged the Empress to make an effort to come with them on horseback, but, knowing that her wound was mortal, and hearing the enemy approach-

CHOUN AND ATO.
(From an Ivory Netsuke.)

TENAGA AND ASHINAGA.
(From an Ivory Netsuke.)

TSUNA AND THE LADY.
(From a Wooden Netsuke.)

(All from Mr. H. S. Trower's collection.)

ing, she bade farewell to Chōun and threw herself into a well which was close by. The enemy proved to be a small party of officers, and Chōun holding the child against his breast with one hand and covering him with his shield, made such a desperate onslaught on the officers that he succeeded in getting away and eventually was able to restore the boy to his father, after many adventures.

Ato grew up to succeed his father as Emperor, and reigned from A.D. 221 to 263

XV.

THE SENNIN AND THE LADY SENDARA.

(India B.C.)

MANY years ago, a certain man named Itkaku, having succeeded in becoming a Sennin, found himself possessing sufficient power to carry into effect his every wish.

When therefore one day he was coming down from his mountain abode and passing through a rocky passage, covered with wet moss, he slipped and fell down in an unexpected, undignified and painful manner, he was naturally exceedingly angry, even though he was a Sennin. Considering therefore that the dragon god, who caused the rain which was the approximate cause of his downfall, was to blame for this unfortunate mischance, the angry Sennin cast a spell on every dragon both great and small, and sealed them all securely in a large and convenient rock. This drastic measure insured the prompt drying up of the aforesaid mossy passage, but, as it stopped the rainfall *everywhere*, also soon caused a famine in the country, all the crops failing for want of water.

The cause of this catastrophe soon transpired, and the king of the country after consultation with his ministers decided to send an embassy to the bruised and wrathful Sennin in his mountain retreat, the embassy to consist of the Lady Sendara, the most beautiful lady of his court, with a large number—some say 500—of attendant beauties whose business it was to be to confuse the poor old Sennin and rob him of his uncanny strength. For this purpose they took up their abode near to the Sennin's hermitage, and paid him frequent calls in the most courteous manner, offering him each time refreshment in the form of a cup of saké or so, the saké at first being very much diluted with water, but increasing in strength at each visit so that at length the curiously unsuspecting Sennin was plied with large quantities of strong spirit, with the inevitable result that he became hopelessly drunk, and then succumbed to the wiles of the Lady Sendara and promptly lost all his magic power. Her object accomplished, the Lady Sendara informed her victim that she was going home, and the Sennin, who had really fallen in love with her, not only said he would accompany her but also offered to carry her on his back all the way to the palace, a feat he accomplished with some difficulty, only to lose his life at the end of the journey, for he was taken immediately by the King's orders and there and then put to death This done, the sealed up dragons once more were free, the spell laid on them being broken, and the wind and rain came and went as ever before the unfortunate Sennin's unlucky fall.

XVI.

SENNIN.

(India, China and Japan)

SENNIN so frequently appear in Japanese art works, that a special page with reference to them will not be out of place in our little work.

The name is formed of two syllables "Sen," meaning "old age, without death," and "Nin" standing for "man;" and the character "Sen" is formed of two letters, signifying "enter" and "mountain." Thus a Sennin means a man who has entered into a mountain. There were nine classes of Sen who could fly up to heaven without dying and, of these, Sennin are the ninth class. The general characteristics of Sennin were, that the colours of their skin did not change nor the skin itself wrinkle, that the sight never grew dim or the physiognomy altered. In addition to this, each Sennin appears to have been able to do some special feat of his own, e.g., one could conjure a miniature horse out of a gourd bottle; another could emit his spiritual essence out of his mouth in the form of a miniature figure of himself, while one, whose representation is particularly popular, was always attended by a large toad. The following recipe for the preparation of a Sennin is from the rule of Oshikio, a Sennin of China ·—" In March pick a young shoot of a sweet chrysanthemum: in June strip the leaves: in September the flower and in December the stem and the roots: each on the day of the tiger in the early part of the month, lay them all to dry in the shade for a hundred days; mix them in equal parts during the dog days, pound them all a thousand times with a wooden mallet, so that they are reduced to powder; mix this powder with honey and out of the mixture make pills, each as large as the seed of the Gotonomi (" Sterenlla Platanifolia ") and then three times a day take seven of the pills. For a hundred days there is little result and then—presuming that an old man is taking the medicine—the white hair begins to turn black again, which it does entirely after a year, in two years the teeth come again, and so on, till at last an old man of 80 becomes quite like a youth."

This recipe does not appear to be applicable to ladies, and we have never heard of any recent case of its being successfully followed.

XVII.

OMORI HIKOHICHI.

(Japan, 14th Century A.D)

HIKOHICHI was, in the middle of the 14th century, an officer of high rank in the Ashikaga army, who, after the great battle of Minatogawa (Hiogo) in which he greatly distinguished himself, was appointed governor over a large and important province. In order to celebrate his accession to this high office, Hikohichi arranged with his family to give a splendid performance of the Sarugaku, an opera-like play, and great numbers of people from neighbouring provinces were attracted to the show.

On one of the several nights during which—according to Japanese custom—the

THE SENNIN AND THE LADY SENDARA.
(*Ivory Netsuke, Mr. G. A. Lee's collection.*)

SABURO AND FISHERMAN.
(*Ivory Netsuke, Mr. H. S. Trower's collection.*)

SHIRO AND BOAR.
(*Ivory Netsuke, Mr. H. S. Trower's collection.*)

play lasted, Hikohichi, who himself appeared therein, was taking a short cut across some fields to the playhouse, when, in the light of the just risen moon, he caught sight of a young girl of seventeen or eighteen years, beautifully dressed and of remarkable loveliness Hikohichi paused in his walk to watch her, thinking that from her appearance she was certainly not a country maiden, and wondering how she came to be out so late, alone and unattended Just then she turned and noticing Hikohichi, came up to him, and in a very sweet and engaging manner said, that she had lost both her companions and her way and did not know what to do, could Hikohichi graciously help her? Hikohichi informed her, in reply, that he would with great pleasure direct her to the theatre, where the great opera was being performed, and added that if she did not happen to have a sajiki (box) engaged for her, he would be greatly delighted to place one at her disposal, if she would be graciously pleased to honour him by accepting it. The lady expressed her extreme delight in accepting Kikohichi's most courteous offer, and turned with the latter in the direction indicated. But after going but a short distance, the lady began to show evident signs of extreme fatigue, and in response to Hikohichi's earnest enquiries admitted that she was too much exhausted to proceed any further. In this dilemma, Hikohichi suggested that if the lady would permit him, he would be delighted to carry her to the playhouse, if she would come, like a child, on his back. The lady readily consented, and Hikohichi, enchanted with his lovely burden, set out again towards the theatre. But his satisfaction was very shortlived, for, on passing under the shadow of an overhanging rock, his load seemed to suddenly increase in weight to an impossible extent, and happening to turn his face up towards the lady, he saw with horror that a strange change had come over her beautiful features. Her lovely eyes had become like a pair of red mirrors, her mouth now reached from ear to ear, the grinning teeth closed on each other like those of a shark, huge eyebrows, as if made of the darkest lacquer, and a pair of horns like those of a young ox sprang from her forehead. Hikohichi, horrified at the ghastly apparition, tried to throw it off, but the demon who had fixed its claws in Hikohichi's top-knot of hair (kami) with the expressed intention of carrying him off to its lair in the mountains, held on firmly, and a desperate struggle ensued, during which they fell down together on the pathway. Hikohichi's shouts at length attracted the attention of some of his retainers, who hurried up with drawn swords, but, as they approached, the demon fled, leaving the unfortunate Hikohichi exhausted with the diabolical contest, and resolved for the future to leave desolate damsels severely alone.

XVIII.

THE AMA AND THE JEWEL.

(Japan).

ONCE upon a time a certain Chinese Emperor sent, as a gift to the Mikado, three very precious jewels, but during their passage to Japan, one of these jewels was stolen by a dragon of the sea, and by him placed in the dragon's palace beneath the waters. On this story being told at Kyōto by the Emperor's messenger, a state minister was despatched on the hopeless errand of recovering the lost jewel. On reaching Sido harbour, near which spot the dragon had stolen the jewel, the minister in question took up his abode there, and settled down, apparently to think out the problem of getting back the lost gem from its present fishy possessors.

In the intervals of the thinking, he employed himself in the agreeable occupation of making love to a pretty Ama (or pearl diver) who bore him a sturdy little son, to whom he became much attached The Ama also, who doated on the child, conceived the idea that he should, in due course, become his father's heir, and as the child grew up her anxiety on this point increased with his growth. At length she broached the idea to her lover, and, after some discussion, the minister agreed that, if the Ama should succeed in recovering the precious lost jewel, her son should be made his lawful heir. Having agreed to these terms, the Ama made all the preparations she had devised for attempting her perilous task of recovering the jewel. With a rope tied round her waist she dived from a ship over the spot where the jewel was lost, and in due course found herself at the entrance of the dragon's palace (Riūgū) which, as well as being apparently impregnable, was guarded also by a number of poisonous and uncanny-looking fish and sea dragons. Although terribly frightened, the Ama, imploring the aid of the gods, and thinking her last moment was come, dashed suddenly into the palace, eluded the guards, who were overfed and unwieldy for lack of exercise, and chancing on the jewel, secured it and fled. But, stupid as his guards were, the great dragon himself was a bit more wide awake, and as soon as he realised his loss started after the daring robber. Although, in answer to her before-determined signal, the Ama was being drawn up to the waiting ship as quickly as possible, she soon saw that unless she took the desperate measure which she had decided upon, should circumstances render it necessary, she would infallibly be caught by the angry dragon, and lose both her life and the jewel: so, drawing a small knife with which she had provided herself, she made a deep incision in her breast and placed in it the precious jewel. The water became instantly red with her blood, and since—as is well-known—the sea dragons detest nothing so much as water defiled with human gore, the baffled dragon at once ceased his pursuit, the Ama was drawn up on board the ship, and, having indicated to the waiting minister where the precious jewel was hidden in her flesh, she fell unconscious, and presently died. Her lover on his return home, religiously kept his promise; the boy became his heir, and eventually succeeded his father in his office of minister as well.

He then raised a temple in the harbour of Shido, to his devoted mother's memory; to which pilgrims resort even at the present day, and which is known as Shidoji.

XIX.-

CHORIO

(China, 3rd Century, B.C.)

About a hundred years before the Shū dynasty came to an end, B.C. 249, a number of the feudal princes, taking advantage of a period of uncertainty and unrest, attacked their neighbours, with the object of each enlarging his own territories. From this state of chaos the Prince of Shin eventually emerged victorious, having succeeded in destroying all his rivals, and he was consequently crowned Emperor, B.C. 246.

Amongst those who were destroyed by Shin was Prince Kan, whose prime minister was Chorio, who in revenge for his master's death attempted to kill the latter's slayer, but, being foiled in this attempt, Chorio fled to Shin's rival Riū Ho (afterwards Emperor of Hung) who, intending to attack and, if possible, destrov their common enemy Shin. Riū Ho cordially welcomed such a clever, useful man as Chorio to his ranks, and the more cordially as the times were then so troublous. Chorio soon became Riū Ho's chief adviser, planning all his tactics and so organising his armies that the eventual success of Riū Ho was to a great extent owing to Chorio's advice and help. When Riū Ho and his colleagues and kinsman, a brave man named Kōwu, had at last succeeded in destroying the government and family of Shin, they fell to quarrelling over the division of the captured lands; and the points at issue were only settled after seventy-two battles or skirmishes, extending over five years.

At the last of these battles which was fought at Kurisan, Kōwu's forces were entirely surrounded by the army of Riū Ho, but the former's body guard consisting of about 8,000 picked men, fought so fiercely and maintained their position with such resolute courage—as the Chinese proverb says " a hard-pressed rat bites even the cat "—that Riū Ho failed to dislodge them before night came, and the fighting ceased. And here Chorio's strategy was employed with extraordinary success. According to his directions, the encompassing army quietly drew off some distance, opening out its ranks and camping in loose order round the compact body of the weary enemy. Chorio then took his dosho, (flute of many reeds) and going down towards the camp of Kōwu, began to play a mournful tune, suggestive of the home life which the stricken soldiers would probably never again know. A pale and waning moon looked down on the dreary scene from a dark and threatening sky, the chilly autumn wind blew the dead leaves over the armour and clothing of the exhausted soldiers, whose supplies having been cut off, were prevented from sleeping by the pangs of hunger and thirst. The desolate scene combined with the lugubrious music proved too much for the hitherto unconquered army. Filled with thoughts of home, first one and then another began to steal quietly out of the camp, and easily evading their sleeping enemies, who had purposely been loosely arranged around them, made their way towards their long deserted homes. When Kōwu woke on the following morning he found his little army had shrunk to about a couple of hundred men. These were soon overpowered and captured and the final victory thus remained with Riū Ho, who became Emperor and reigned until B.C 195: while his dynasty lasted until A.D. 220

XX.

YORIMASA'S LUCKY SHOT.

Many centuries ago, in the imperial palace at Kyōto, it was observed by the courtiers and guard about the palace, that about the hour of the ushi (i.e., 2 a.m.) every night, a small black cloud came quickly up from the south-east, and alighted on the palace roof beneath which the Emperor Konoye lay sleeping, and that, as the cloud settled on the roof, his majesty started in his sleep, and gave signs of being in great distress. Night after night this weird visitation continued, until the Emperor's health was most seriously affected, and the court became a very dismal place indeed The doctors could do nothing, the prayers of the priests were offered in vain, the only result being that now, from the cloud came horrible sounds, as from some diabolical spirit hidden therein, and the Emperor grew still weaker At last the ministers, in consultation, determined to send for Minamoto Yorimasa, who was reputed to be possessed of special cunning and dexterity in dealing with similar uncanny visitants. In due course he arrived at the palace, accompanied by his Kerai, a private soldier, named Ino Hayata, with his bow and arrows, the state of affairs was communicated to him, and he determined to test the matter that very night. Taking, therefore, up his position as near as possible to the place on the roof on which the cloud always alighted, he waited events. As the hour of the ox was struck by the watchers of the night, the cloud appeared as usual on the south-eastern horizon, and rapidly approached the palace, emitting the usual horrible cries. Yorimasa, undaunted, quietly observed the cloud, and arriving at the conclusion that it certainly shrouded some malignant creature, silently invoked the god of war, fitted an arrow on his bow, and with the determination in his own mind that he would not survive his failure in this enterprise, he pulled the bow—as they say in Japan—" to the full moon," and let fly the deadly arrow Even as it sped, he felt sure that it would reach its mark, and sure enough, with a horrible scream the black cloud dissolved, and down from the palace roof fell a writhing form. Drawing his dagger and rushing forward, Yorimasa's faithful attendant stabbed deeply nine times, and, lights being brought, the quarry was found to be a fearsome monster known as a Nuye, having, with a monkey's head, a badger's body, with the legs of a tiger, and a venomous snake for a tail. His evil genius being thus destroyed, the Emperor immediately recovered, and Yorimasa received much honour and applause for his intrepidity and skill.

XXI.

SOGA GORO AND ASAHINA SABURO.

(Japan, 12th Century A D)

In the 4th year of Kenkiu (A.D. 1193) Wada Yoshimori, a Daimio of Kamakura, came to Oiso, being with his family and household on his way to Shimozuke. Then, as now, Oiso was a very fashionable seaside resort, and many Yukuns—who were girls specially trained to sing and dance—a variety, in fact, of Geisha, were to be found at its numerous tea-houses and inns. During his stay here, Yoshimori gave a great feast in one of the largest of the tea-houses, to his friends and attendants, who numbered about eighty: and, to amuse these guests, some thirty Yukuns were engaged. But when these little people appeared in due course, Yoshimori soon perceived that the gem of the collection, a certain O Tora San, was missing. Now O Tora San was a very well known person indeed, so her absence from the entertainment was felt to be a slight on both host and guests, and Yoshimori consequently looked very glum indeed.

It happened, however, that Tora was in love with Soga Jūro—who was the elder brother of Soga Goro—and on this particular occasion was entertaining the former on her own account, at the inn where she lodged, instead of turning up to amuse Yoshimori's family and guests. But Yoshimori was quite well aware of the cause of her absence, and calling over his third son, Asahina Saburo, he bade him go round at once to the Tora abode, and invite her to come immediately to his party, with a special injunction to accept no refusal or excuse. Now everybody who happened to overhear this message realized that the fat was indeed all in the fire, since Jūro being a Bushi (i e., one who is entitled to wear two swords) would necessarily regard it as a point of honour not to permit the girl to keep her engagement with Yoshimori. The news of Saburo's mission appears to have preceded him to Tora's inn, for the innkeeper was able to warn Tora and Jūro that Saburo was on his way, with a pressing invitation for the pleasure of her company. When Jūro heard this, he realized that whether she wanted to go or not, it was clearly *his* duty to prevent her, and then he had time to remember that he had promised his brother, Goro, to make, in the immediate future, all the necessary arrangements for hunting down and killing an enemy of their late father (which indeed was successfully accomplished a little later on, when the Shogun Yoritomo held a hunting party on Fuji-Yama), and for a time he was considerably puzzled how to act, but eventually decided that, if Saburo had indeed the temerity to attempt to oppose him, he would necessarily be compelled to do his best to cut Saburo in half.

But on the other hand Saburo also had thought the matter out, and as he too realized that Jūro could not, as the son of a brave soldier and himself a Bushi, let O Tora San go, without a desperate attempt to prevent her, he decided to take his own line in the matter, and on arriving at the inn, and being received by Tora and Jūro, Saburo in the most courteous manner addressed the lady, saying, "May I beg you to be pleased to come, to our banquet, O Tora San, and, at my father's most special invitation, will your honourable guest come also?" Jūro was quite taken aback by this unlooked for courtesy, and, forgetting entirely his bloodthirsty intentions regarding Saburo, after a pause, replied, "Many thanks, we are delighted to come," and they returned to the feast, where the beautiful guest was most warmly welcomed. When the banquet was at its height and the saké bottles were passing round, Yoshimori asked O Tora San to give her saké cup to the one present whom she most admired. Tora laughed, and half turned towards Yoshimori himself, and then drew back and begging the others to excuse her, handed the cup to Jūro, who took it without any show of hesitation. Yoshimori smiled sarcastically and remarked, "If I had been twenty years younger, I might have had her cup."

They sat so long over the feast that the news of Saburo's setting out to compel Tora's attendance thereat, reached Goro—Jūro's younger brother—at his home in Soga, and the latter fearing mischief did not even wait to saddle a horse, but jumping on one, bare-backed, in the armour he happened to be wearing, covered the two miles to Oiso, and reached the tea-house within a very few minutes Here he learnt that the danger which he feared was practically over· but, thinking that it might perhaps break out again ere the feast came to an end, he secretly entered the garden of the tea-house and took his stand on the verandah just outside the shoji (paper covered sliding door) at the back of his brother's seat, so that if anyone assaulted the latter he might be close at hand to assist him, and, drawing his sword he wetted the mekugi (bamboo rivet, which fastens the blade to the handle: to wet this is to tighten it) and waited for events. Saburo, inside, happened to catch sight of Goro's shadow, and, simulating intoxication, pushed open the shoji and intentionally staggered against Goro, who was standing like a Nio (one of the two gigantic figures who guard temple gates), and catching hold of Goro's kusazuri (skirts of the cuirass, attached thereto by a number of thick silk cords) cried out, " Hullo, here my good friend, won't you come in, please," and pulled at the armour to drag Goro in, but the latter did not stir, and Saburo said, "Well, even if you are a rock, you are less than six feet high, so here goes for another pull to get you in," and so saying, he tugged with all his might, and still Goro stood like a tree, while all the assembled guests crowded round to watch this extraordinary contest. Goro still standing, and Saburo still pulling, at length with a crack all the silk cords gave way at once, and Saburo fell back crashing on the floor and still holding tight to the torn kusazuri, while Goro was seen to be still erect, never having budged from his first position. A roar of laughter greeted Saburo's fall, and Goro with hearty congratulations was pressed to join the feast.

The extraordinary strength and endurance displayed by both these young men on this occasion, made a great sensation in their own lifetime, and ever since, have been the subject of wonder and admiration to their countrymen. Representations of their feat have been reproduced on countless works of art, amongst which, perhaps, the furniture of swords is the favourite medium of display, though netsukes and colour-prints cannot be much less fully represented.

XXII.

KOJIMA TAKANORI.

(Japan, 14th Century A.D.)

THE Emperor Godaigo Tenno, who reigned in Japan in the first part of the 14th century, had with the civil officers of his court—in the absence of all the Daimios—prepared a plan, by which the power of the dominant and disloyal Hojo family, who were in revolt against Kyōto, the Shogun's deputy in Kamakura, was to be dissipated and the family itself destroyed, and in order to develop this plan, he sent secret instructions to the loyal Daimios. But these instructions came by mischance to the knowledge of Takatoki, the head of the Hojo clan, who immediately decided to kidnap the Emperor, and place him well out of the way, in the island of Oki, to the north-west of the empire. The defenceless Emperor fell an easy prey to Takatoki's armed forces, and with a couple of equerries and a lady-in-waiting, was hurried off in secret from Kyōto, one day in March, 1332, on the road to the isle of Oki.

Now, one of the families, who, in obedience to the Mikado's secret order, had

KIKUJIDO.
Ivory Netsuke,
Mr. H. S. Trower's collection.)

YORIMASA.

INOHAYATA AND NUYE.
(Pouch Mountings,
Mr. G. A. Lee's collection.)

begun to collect troops to serve against the Hojo, was that of Kojima in the Bizen Province, whose feudal head was Saburo Takanori The latter, however, soon heard of the failure of the enterprise, and with the troops already raised, determined to attack the Hojo army and rescue the Mikado. For this purpose he led his men to a road by Mount Fūnasakayama, on the road to Oki, but Takatoki, probably suspecting an ambush, led the Mikado's escort round another unsuspected path, and passed on unmolested, so Saburo's hope and intention became as useless as a froth of water. Then it struck Saburo that although he was unable actually to rescue the Emperor, it might be possible to send the latter some message or communication, of such a nature as to free his mind from anxiety, and assure him that he still had loyal friends working for him against his enemies Saburo therefore disguised himself as a peasant, wearing a straw rain coat and hat, and approached the wayside inn in which one evening the Mikado was lodged But he soon ascertained that, owing to the precautions taken to preserve the imperial prisoner's seclusion, there was no chance of communicating with him.

Still when all was quiet at night, Saburo succeeded in stealing unobserved into the garden at the back of the house, where he concluded the Emperor's bedroom was, and with his knife peeled off some of the bark of a cherry tree there, and on the smooth place thus provided, wrote a couplet of verses to the following effect:—

"Kosen was not by heaven forsaken,
"Hanrei may still be sent to you,"—

in allusion to a certain King of China, Kosen, who, being defeated and taken prisoner by his enemy named Fuso, his cause was taken up by his minister named Hanrei, and, so vigorously by the latter, that Fuso was eventually defeated and killed, and Kosen liberated.

The following morning the Mikado saw the writing and understood the message, and indeed in the event, Saburo worked in the provinces so enthusiastically for the Mikado's cause, that by the following year the latter was victorious and the Hojo family was destroyed.

XXIII.

KIDOMARU.

(Japan, 10th Century A.D.)

KIDOMARU was the name of a young divinity student—as he would be styled in Europe—who at the end of the tenth century lived in Hiyezan. Instead of demurely continuing his abstruse studies, he suddenly abandoned the idea of ever becoming a Sojo (or Bishop) and, by way of a complete change of air and occupation, started life afresh as a highway robber, and soon succeeded, by his exploits in the outlying districts of Kyōto, in considerably upsetting the peace and security of the worthy citizens.

As soon however as the matter reached the ears of Minamoto Yorinobu he sent off his Kerai (private officers and guards) to secure the young ruffian, which they promptly did, and lodged him safely in the prison. The day after this event, Yorinobu's brother Raiko paid him a visit, and seeing in the prison cage a remarkably sinister looking prisoner, asked who this was. "The youngster's name is Kidomaru," replied

Yorinobu, " we nabbed him only yesterday, and as there are several serious charges against him, if he is convicted, he will get a pretty severe sentence." " He's certainly got a very nasty face," said Raiko, " and he looks unusually strong, if I were you I would tie him up tightly and keep a good watch over him too." Yorinobu took his brother's advice, but, in defiance of all their precautions, Kidomaru escaped and managed to get clear away that very night, and having heard the advice given to his brother by Raiko, was filled with rage against the latter. Some little time afterwards, Raiko had occasion to pay a visit to the Kuramayama temple, and passing on his way through Ichiharano field, his attendant called his attention to a dead ox, lying in a distant corner of the field, surrounded by cows. As he watched it, an idea occurred to the attendant that some evil threatened his master, and on mentioning this idea to Raiko the latter drew an arrow and shot it towards the dead ox. As he did so, Kidomaru, who had concealed himself inside it, emerged from the carcase, and rushed towards Raiko, but on approaching was easily caught and killed.

XXIV.

THE BLIND TORTOISE.

(A parable from the Buddhist sacred book, Hoke-Kyo.)

A certain tortoise, having a single eye situated in the middle of its *under* side, lives at the bottom of the sea. Once in three thousand years this tortoise rises to the surface and floats thereon, but having no eyes in its head it does not see the sun, unless it would happen to meet with a floating board in which there was a hole pierced, and that getting on this board the tortoise should place himself so that his single eye was opposite the hole, and then it should happen that a heavy gust of wind should blow the tortoise and the wood right over, so that then the tortoise with its single eye might really see the sun.

Thus, to say that a certain event is likely to happen as often as the one eyed tortoise sees the sun, is tantamount to saying that it is not likely to happen at all.

For, the tortoise can only come to the surface once in three thousand years, and if there is no piece of wood, it must return to the bottom of the sea immediately; and even if there is a piece of wood, and this has no hole in it, or if the hole is not so placed that the single eye of the tortoise when standing on the wood is opposite to the hole, or even, when all these contingencies are satisfactory, if no sudden gust of wind occurs, the tortoise still loses its sight of the sun, and not only thus, but if the tortoise happens to come to the surface when the wood and the wind and all is satisfactory but when it is either night or a cloudy day, it must wait again for another three thousand years before it can come to the surface again.

XXV.

MANZAI.

In ancient times in old Japan it was the custom, on the 14th day of the new year, for the men to assemble in the garden of the Seirioden palace in Kyōto and chant a song, which, from the closing words thereof, was known as "Banzai-raku" (i.e., literally—"ten thousand years' comfort ") afterwards abbreviated to " Manzai," having a similar meaning. This ceremony was repeated by the women a couple of days later.

From the early part of the Ashikaga Period (A.D. 1336-1573) dancers have been permitted to wear the Eboshi and Shitatare, that is an official hat, a mitre and robe, and from the earliest time down to the restoration of the Mikado in A.D 1868, certain dancers used to visit Kyōto every year, coming from the province of Yamato, and being known therefore as Yamato Manzai. On the east of Japan, the Manzai came to Yedo from the province of Mikawa, during the whole period of the Tokugawa Shogunate, i.e., from A.D. 1603 to 1867, their songs and dances being similar to those of Yamato. Both these public celebrations were abolished for a time, early in the present reign, but within the last few years these old customs have again been publicly, in a rather modified form, revived; the dancers appearing on New Year's Day, and going from house to house with fan and tsūzūmi (hand drum, played with the fingers) and generally receiving from the inhabitants some small coin, as an acknowledgement of their little entertainment. For there is no Society for the Suppression of this sort of thing in Japan, and strolling players are generally made welcome

---

XXVI.

TAKEDA SHINGEN AND UYESUGI KENSHIN.

(Japan, 16th Century A.D.)

The dynasty of Ashikaga Shoguns, which began in A.D. 1336, came to an end in 1573, and a long period of civil war ensued, the most powerful and the bravest of the great feudal chiefs contending with each other to gain the supreme power in Japan. This age of turmoil is designated by Japanese historians, "the fighting period."

Amongst these contending chiefs, Oda Nobunaga was apparently on the point of definitely obtaining the mastery, when, in 1582, he was assassinated by his follower, Mitsuhide. But Nobunaga was swiftly avenged, Mitsuhide falling at the hands of his colleague Hideyoshi—a little later famous in history, by the name of "Taiko"—who succeeded where his chief had failed, and eventually became the recognised head of the contending feudal powers in Japan.

Among the chiefs who fought in these unfortunate wars was Murakami Yoshikiyo, who governed an extensive estate in the province of Shinano, situated in the most central and mountainous part of Japan, having on the south, in the province of Kai, the estate of the brave Takeda Shingen, and on the north in the province of Echigo, the daring soldier Uyesugi Kenshin as his neighbours. Yoshikiyo was opposed by Shingen, and, after desperate fighting, was defeated and his estate seized by his victorious neighbour Flying northwards, Yoshikiyo, his power broken and his forces demoralized, took refuge with Kenshin, begging the latter's assistance to eject Shingen and recover his lost estate. Kenshin was a chivalrous soldier, and although then in middle life, yielded to his guest's importunity, and concentrated his own forces on the frontier of Yoshikiyo's estate by Kawanaka-jima, in the 16th year of Tenbun, A.D. 1547. Shingen, nothing loathe, joined battle with him, and though a desperate conflict ensued each side held its own. Time after time the struggle was renewed on the same spot, but neither side could outmatch its opponent, and for fourteen years the rival forces faced each other and fought, exhausting every device, meeting stratagem by stratagem, clever attack by more clever defence, until at last the hopeless struggle ended in a mutual arrangement between the contending generals, Shingen and Kenshin: and in 1561 the campaign was brought to a close. This extraordinary engagement has excited the enthusiasm of Japanese writers, who delight in describing the details of the various battles and skirmishes, the arrangement of the troops and the tactics of the generals, citing it as a sort of object lesson of the whole science and art of war.

Although the fighting was so desperate and so prolonged, the conflict appears to have been conducted with extraordinary forbearance and courtesy on both sides; for, as the Japanese say, "their minds were as clear as a mirror," and they bore no resentment against each other. The following incident occurred during the course of the conflict, and has quite a flavour of Malory about it, being much noted by Japanese historians as a good example of "Bushido." Shingen's estate did not produce any salt, and this necessary commodity was therefore supplied to him from a province to the south of his own. On one occasion the governor of this province having picked a quarrel with Shingen, promptly stopped the supply of salt to the latter's country, and thereby reduced the inhabitants to great distress The circumstance coming to Kenshin's knowledge, he sent a message to Shingen, saying, "We are competing in military affairs, but I hear that your enemy on the south is annoying you by stopping the supply of salt to your people, which is truly a dishonourable and inhuman act Though it is not so convenient as the former source of your supply, you may freely obtain salt from my country," and, true to his word, Kenshin continued to furnish his enemy with the precious mineral at the ordinary market price.

In 1573, one day when Kenshin was at dinner, news arrived of the death of his old opponent, Shingen, and throwing down his hashi (chop sticks) Kenshin regretfully exclaimed, "I have lost my good enemy, and have no one now to compete with me on equal terms." He survived his late opponent nearly five years, dying in 1578.

The illustration (from an 18th century sword guard by Nara Shigechika) represents the following incident in the long struggle. Kenshin, mounted and armed with a long sword, suddenly, at the head of a troop, made a successful dash on Shingen's encampment. The latter was unprepared for Kenshin's sudden onslaught, and being unable to draw his own weapon, could only defend himself with his great iron fan or "toūchiwa," with which he parried three terrible strokes from his enemy's blade, receiving however a serious wound in his thumb. By this time a retainer had come to his assistance, and Kenshin withdrew, satisfied with having caught his enemy unprepared: and the desultory fighting ceased.

XXVII.

UJIGAWA.

(Jan., 1184 A.D.)

WHILE Yoritomo was at Kamakura by Yedo, completing his plans for securing the

A KAMAKURA JUDGE.
(*Wood Netsuke,*
Mr. H. S. Trower's collection.)

YOSHISADA AT
INAMURAGA SAKI.
(*Ivory Netsuke,*
Mr. H. S. Trower's collection.)

KIDŌMARU.
(*Ivory Netsuke,*
Mr. H. Seymour Trower's collection.)

Shogunate, his cousin Yoshinaka made a sudden attack on Kyōto, which was then the chief stronghold of the Heishi—or Taira family—taking it by storm and driving its defenders out, the latter fleeing towards Hiogo and the Inland Sea. Yoshinaka thus acquired a position in which it was possible to compel the court party at Kyōto to make him Shogun, and as soon as he thus obtained the title, he set to work to do exactly as he pleased in the old city, becoming insolent and cruel, not only to the imperial family who were entirely in his power, but also towards the clergy and citizens, until the latter began to regret even the bad old days of Heishi domination. The court at length realizing that, as the Japanese proverb says, while driving out a tiger from the front gate, they had let in a wolf by the back, secretly sent a message to Yoritomo at Kamakura, begging him to come and destroy Yoshinaka, before going to engage the Heishi. Yoritomo in reply arranged that his two brothers, Yoshitsune and Noriyori, should proceed with an army against Yoshinaka, and the expedition was speedily organised. Now at this time Yoritomo had with him two favourite horses, remarkable for swiftness and endurance, and named respectively Iketsuki and Sūrūsūmi. Kajiwara Kagesūye, one of Yoritomo's chief officers, who was to go with the army to Kyōto, when taking leave of Yoritomo begged that he might have the horse Iketsuki to ride on this expedition.

Now this horse was believed to be the best of the two, so Yoritomo while excusing himself from granting the other's request, saying that he must keep one of the horses for himself in case of emergency, offered Kajiwara Sūrūsūmi, and the offer was accepted.

Shortly afterwards, Kajiwara's colleague Sasaki Takatsūna also had an audience of Yoritomo to bid him farewell, and for some unknown reason Yoritomo spontaneously offered to Takatsūna the very horse he had just previously denied to Kajiwara. Takatsūna was overwhelmed with gratitude at the great favour shewn to him, and after thanking his master most sincerely, added, "I will cross the Ujigawa* riding Iketsuki, ahead of the whole army. If I live I shall be the first across, for if anyone

* The chief defence of Kyōto, the passage of which had been a subject of anxious discussion by the generals and staff.

else succeeds in crossing before me, I shall not live to witness his triumph," and his confident tone was generally remarked upon by those who heard him.

When the army arrived at the river Ujigawa, Kajiwara and Takatsūna, without telling each other, both determined to be the first to cross the river in front of them, and very early on the following morning they met on the banks of the river, each being mounted, and having galloped down to a spot which presented itself as a favourable starting place. The to-do occasioned by their early rising had roused the rest of the army, who watched the result of the race with the greatest interest. Both were young and gallant soldiers, from that eastern portion of the empire from whence the bravest troops were ever drawn, and the horses they rode were worthy of their riders. Kajiwara obtained a start of some thirty feet when Takatsūna who was behind called out, "I say, general, don't forget that this is the strongest and most rapid stream in the whole of this part of the country, and see, your horse's girth is loose, you ought for your own sake to tighten it." Kajiwara, holding his bow in his teeth, began to tighten the girth, and while he was thus occupied, Takatsūna whipped into the river and began to swim across, promptly followed by his disgusted colleague, who naturally felt that he had been cheated into making way for his wily rival. Determined not to be outdone, Kajiwara in his turn called out to Takatsūna, " Don't be in too much of a hurry yourself or you will come to grief. There are probably ropes laid across the river out of sight." Takatsūna only replied by drawing his sword and cutting into the water as he urged his way across, and the start that he obtained he kept, reaching the bank directly opposite to the point of starting, some time before his rival, who was carried by the stream some distance further down. As soon as he set foot on shore, Takatsūna called out in a loud voice, " The vanguard of the army at Ujigawa, I, Sasaki Shiro Takatsūna, the fourth son of Sasaki Saburo Yoshihide, the ninth descendant of the Emperor Uta Tenno." And so the army was led towards Kyōto, and Takatsūna justified his boast to Yoritomo.

MANZAI.

*(Ivory Netsuke,
Messrs. Yamanaka & Co.'s collection.)*

SHOJŌ.

*(Lacquered on Ivory Netsuke,
Mr. H. S. Trower's collection.*

THE BLIND TORTOISE.

*(Ivory Netsuke,
Mr. G. Ambrose Lee's collection.)*

XXVIII.

YOJŌ.

(China, 400 B.C.

YOJŌ at the commencement of the story was a retainer of a certain prince named Hanchu Koshi, being certainly then in a very inferior—not to say menial—position, in the latter's court, but what this position exactly was is not recorded. Hanchu Koshi had the misfortune to have a serious difference of opinion with Chihakū, by whom he was put to death, and Yojō passed with other goods and chattels to his late master's successful destroyer. Chihakū treated this new retainer with extreme cordiality, gave him an excellent position in the household and always referred to him as one worthy of respect and honour. But Chihakū was destined to come to a similar violent end to that which he had doomed Hanchu Koshi, for in due course a certain knight named Chojōshi, conspired with two other neighbouring knights against Chihakū, defeated him, and not only captured and put him to death but also involved all his blood relations in the same fate, and then divided his estate into three parts, each successful conspirator keeping a part. Chojōshi appears to have had some special grievance against Chihakū, for he took his skull, had it lacquered over, and used it as a drinking vessel.

On the death of Chihakū, Yojō managed to escape to the mountains and to hide himself there. And musing somewhat to this effect, "A gentleman who recognises the obligations of honour, should be ready to give his life for one who has honoured him, just as naturally as a woman adorns herself to please one who loves her. Chihakū honoured me, though so unworthy: I must therefore revenge his death and then die, for only thus can I discharge the debt of gratitude I owe to Chihakū, and ensure that my soul be not ashamed to meet his after my death." With this intention, Yojō disguised himself, changed his name, and went down to the palace of Chojōshi, where he was successful in joining himself to a body of prisoners condemned to hard labour, who were engaged in making some alterations in a private apartment adjoining Chojōshi's own dwelling rooms. It chanced that Chojōshi had occasion to enter this apartment and something rousing

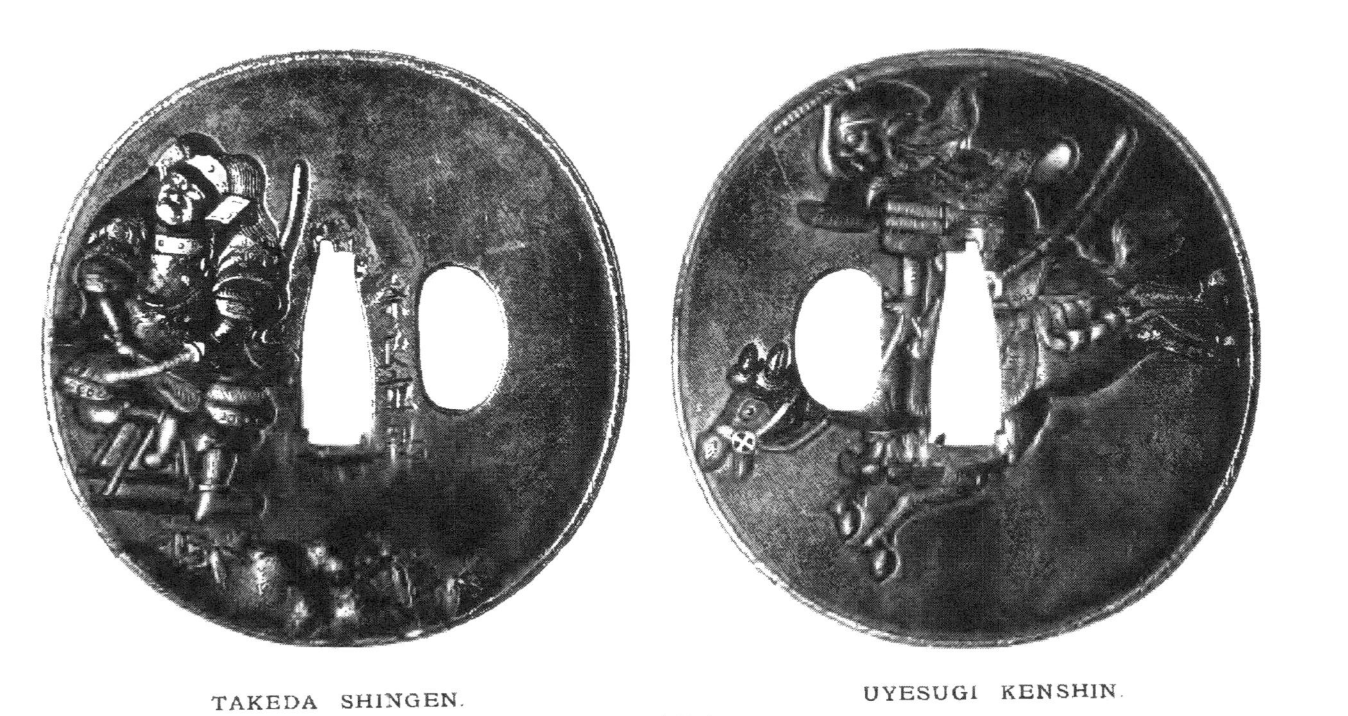

TAKEDA SHINGEN. UYESUGI KENSHIN.

(Shakudo Tsuba,
From Mr. G. Ambrose Lee's collection.)

his suspicions, he suddenly called to the guards and ordered all the prisoners at work there to be rigorously searched. This was done, and a dagger was found concealed on Yojō, who without hesitation said to the king, "I brought this intending to kill you in revenge for the death of my late master Chihakū." At these words the attendants raised their weapons to kill him, but Chojōshi stopped them, saying, "He is indeed a faithful servant; for, since his master has no successors who could reward him for his fidelity, he has nothing to gain, from a wise man of the world's point of view, by such an act of revenge," and he had Yojō set at liberty, remarking that he himself would take good care in the future that this jealous and too faithful person should have no second chance of coming near enough to kill him.

Yojō departed, but had then no idea of giving up his revengeful pursuit; so he proceeded to stain himself all over to appear as if he were a leper, and by drinking a certain mild poison he was able to alter his voice, and the two changes together constituted such a successful disguise, that when he went out begging in the streets of the city nobody recognized him; even his wife—from whom he was separated—passing him, unaware of his identity. But it happened that one day a certain man with whom he had been on terms of great intimacy, passed him in the street, and being aware of Yojō's intentions, and seeing something familiar in the shabbily dressed individual who slouched by, stopped him and said, "Are you not my old friend, Yojō?" The latter replied, "Yes, I am," and his friend then said, "Would it not be easier for one who is as clever as you are to become a follower of Chojōshi, and then when you have by your assiduity lulled his suspicions to rest, to find some opportunity of killing him quietly, rather than disfigure and injure yourself as you are doing?" "I know that I seem to be going a very roundabout and difficult way to work," replied Yojō, "but you know it requires two minds to serve one master, and I do not care to contemplate killing Chojōshi after having been in his service, so the reason why I am taking this devious path to my revenge, is that I may shame those who would serve a master without loyalty towards him, and that my honest dealing in this matter may serve as an example to future generations."

Soon after this, when Chojōshi was crossing a bridge in the city his horse was frightened by some moving object, and when he ordered his escort to search and see what was wrong, they found Yojō armed and concealed in the wood-work beneath the bridge. Chojōshi without a trace of anger addressed him saying, " Why are you so bent on killing me, out of revenge for Chihakū, who was indeed your master, but who himself destroyed Hanchu Koshi who was your first master: when you not only did not kill the latter's slayer but even entered his service?" Yojō replied, "True, but while I was in Hanchu Koshi's service, he treated me merely as an ordinary menial servant: so, on his death, having been so regarded, I felt under no obligation whatever to avenge him; but Chihakū took me as a personal attendant, treating me ever with honour, respect and confidence, hence I am, in endeavouring to avenge his death, merely humbly acknowledging the obligations imposed upon me by my late lord's kindness and condescension towards me." Chojōshi hearing this reply sighed and said, "You have done enough for your master, and I too did enough in overlooking your former attempt against me. Prepare to meet your end, for I shall not forgive you again," and he signed to the guards to secure Yojō preparatory to putting him to death. The latter remarked, " It is a faithful subject's duty to die for his sovereign's honour. You set me free, it is true, after my last attempt against you, and all people speak highly of your wisdom. I am, of course, ready to meet the death I expected as the punishment of this attempt, but before I die, I beg you, give me one of your garments so that I may stab it and that this may represent my revenge consummated upon you, and that I may therefore so die, feeling no illwill towards you as I pass into another life." Chojōshi, acknowledging Yojō's loyalty and integrity, took off his coat and gave it to the latter, who thanked him very respectfully, and taking the coat stabbed it deeply three times, exclaiming, " Now, I have repaid Chihakū's kindness towards me," and immediately afterwards he deliberately stabbed himself. Yojō's devotion and self-sacrifice were admired and applauded by all, and no story of heroism is more popular even at the present day in heroic Japan.

XXIX.

GENTOKU'S RIDE.

(China, 3rd Century A.D)

GENTOKU was a descendant of the fourth generation of the Emperor Keitei of the Eastern Hung dynasty. Although of Royal blood, he began life in the humble position of a shoemaker, and amongst the neighbours was well known for his affection for and attention towards his widowed mother. His great strength, and his extraordinary height—for he is said to have been seven feet six inches tall, with arms that, as he stood upright, reached below his knees—soon, however, marked him out for success in what was, at the end of the 2nd century, A.D. in China, practically the only road to success, i.e., the profession of a soldier; and when he was instrumental in bringing about the defeat of the uprising of the "Yellow ribbon rebels"—so called from their use of yellow ribbons as a badge—he was rewarded with the title and office of Governor of Yoshu. But on his defeat by Soso in A.D 207 he was driven out of Yoshu, and being homeless took refuge with an old relative named Riu Hio, by whom he was welcomed, and who assigned him quarters in a neighbouring castle, where Gentoku accordingly took up his abode. But, unfortunately, this arrangement did not at all suit Hio's wife and her brother (who was a commander in the army) who both regarded the giant Gentoku as a sort of wild beast, whom it would be best to kill while he was safely caged up. With this end in view, they prepared a great banquet, to which they intended to invite the beast in question, and then put him to death. Gentoku, unsuspecting, accepted the invitation and at the appointed time rather disconcerted his would-be-murderers by turning up with an armed escort of some three hundred fighting men under the command of the brave general Choun (vide "Choun and Ato"). On his arrival he was secretly informed, by Hio's staff-officer Iseki, that the banquet was really a pitfall, his destruction being intended, and that an army of about 9,000 men in three divisions was posted on three sides of Hio's castle to prevent his escape, while the fourth side was the river Dankei, which being of great width, and with a very strong and rapid current, effectually, as it was believed, closed

KOJIMA TAKANORI.

(*Shibuichi Tsuba,*
Mr. W. L. Behrens's collection.)

UJIGAWA.

his escape towards the west. As soon as he realized his position, Gentoku, without a moment's delay, decided to attempt to escape across the river, and without waiting to inform his escort, he threw himself on to his favourite horse Tekiro and bolted towards the water. As soon as it became obvious that the bird was flown, a picked body of horsemen was detached in pursuit, but Gentoku, although he knew the apparent hopelessness of his task, decided in his own mind that "destiny is determined by heaven" gave rein to his good horse and dashed into the river. No one of his pursuers felt himself called upon to attempt to follow the fugitive into the swirling waters, and, fate favouring the bold, Gentoku safely negotiated the dangerous passage and gained the opposite bank, thus escaping the snare so carefully set for him.

After many desperate battles he at length, in A.D. 221, obtained the sovereignty of Shoku, and died in the following year. His perilous escape is a frequent subject of illustration.

XXX.

NITTA YOSHISADA AT INAMURAGA SAKI HARBOUR.

(Japan, 14th Century A.D.)

At the beginning of the fourteenth century, some nine generations had passed away since Hojō Tokimasa—whose sister married the first Shogun, Yoritomo (A.D. 1148 to 1199)—had on the latter's death considerably encroached, under the name of Shikken (i.e., Regent), on the Shogun's governing powers. The ninth descendant of this Hojō, then living, was Takatoki, destined to be the last of his line. He was a fierce, lawless and cruel man, and the eyes of many of the Daimios, outraged by his excesses and disloyalty, turned towards the Mikado, Godaigo Tenno, then nominally reigning, looking to him to devise some measures to determine a state of affairs which was rapidly involving the country in ruin. Having for some time borne Takatoki's oppression with exemplary patience, Godaigo believing that the time of deliverance was at hand, sent secret directions to all the friendly Daimios to raise all their available forces, and take other specified steps towards the end in view. One of these Daimios, the gallant Nitta Yoshisada, promptly raised his loyal flag, as near as possible to the Hojō base at Kamakura, and was joined by a number of other loyal Daimios. At the head of the forces Yoshisada inflicted several defeats on the Hojō armies, and at length came up to them at Inamuraga Saki harbour, the last defence of Kamakura, facing the sea. Here he found facing him, across the arm of the sea which formed the harbour, a heavily armed fort protected by sakamogi, or strong entanglements and outworks formed of felled trees, defended by skilled archers: while on the left, or land side, of the harbour, were hundreds of boats full of other archers within bowshot, should the attacking forces endeavour to advance in that direction. Yoshisada with the other chiefs of the loyal army made a careful survey of the situation, and arrived at the conclusion, so well had the defences been arranged, that they were practically impregnable, Yoshisada remarking that without boats, unless they had wings to fly, it was impossible to cross the sea. He had, however, pledged himself to attack Kamakura by a certain date, while other divisions of the loyal army made a simultaneous attack in another direction, so he determined to attempt the impossible. Dismounting, he laid aside his war helmet, and going down to the beach, he prayed as follows:—"I, Nitta Yoshisada, supplicate you, O gods of the sea, ancestors of this Emperor of ours, now reigning, who from you inherits the lordship of the sea as well as of the land. Regard, I pray you, your successor, exiled* and unhappy, in the power and at the mercy of his cruel and disloyal enemies. For my own sake and for myself I ask nothing, but help me, as a loyal servant of Godaigo Tenno, to destroy the traitorous Hojō and to restore peace to his distracted country. O gods of the sea and dragons who live therein, examine and prove my loyalty, and finding it sincere, be pleased to draw away the waters, that our loyal army may cross and meet the enemies of thy sacred descendant." And as he finished his prayer, Yoshisada unfastened his splendid gold mounted tachi (that is, long slung sword) and threw it as an offering into the waves.

On that very night, just as the great golden moon sank behind the western hills,

* In the Island of Oki—*Vide* the story of "Kojima Takanori."

YOJŌ.

(From a Wooden Netsuke in Mr. W. L. Behrens's collection.)

CHORIO.

(Ivory Netsuke, Mr. H. S. Trower's collection.)

GENTOKU'S RIDE.

(From a Shibuichi Sword Guard in Mr. G. Ambrose Lee's collection.)

the tide drew away from the shore carrying with it all the host of armed boats, to a distance of more than twenty cho (i.e., a mile and a half), and, over the hard sands to the great city, streamed the forces of the loyalists. The enemy were defeated, Kamakura captured, and the Hojō destroyed.

XXXI.

SHUN KWAN.

(Japan, circa 1177 A.D.)

DURING this period in Japan, the Heishi family were in possession of almost supreme power at the Emperor's Court at Kyōto; the family estates comprised more than half of Japan itself, and its members filled the highest positions both in the civil and military establishments, at the Court and in politics. And not only that, but the head of the family, Kiyomori, son of that Tadamori who had received such great favours from the retired Emperor, being given high rank and position at Court (vide "Tadamori and the Oil Thief"), was exceedingly turbulent and overbearing, and had even succeeded in obliging the Emperor to marry his daughter and make her Empress. It was equivalent to social extinction at this period, in the Court, if one was not in some way related to the Heishi family.

But, as the proverb says, "a proud man doesn't last long," and as it happened, some fifteen years before the century closed, the Heishi family had been entirely wiped out* by their opponents, the Genji, and left behind them in history nothing but tales of pride and cruelty.

Shun Kwan was the administrator of the Hosshoji temple, but taking a great interest in politics, he joined himself to a party of the Genji, whose leader was the retired Emperor who had been compelled by the Heishi to abdicate, being unable to endure the latter's iron domination. The party in question was mainly composed of expelled ministers and generals, with many monks, clergy, and court gentlemen, and on a certain day they agreed to meet together on a mountain outside Kyōto, to formulate a plan to circumvent and destroy the hated Heishi.

---

*Vide "Saburo and the Fisherman" and "Ujigawa."

The meeting took place: but a traitor had given information regarding it to Kiyomori, and the latter, at the head of a great force of armed men surrounded the place where the plotters had assembled and eventually captured all their chiefs and leaders.

Rigorous confinement or exile was the lot of all the captives, and with a couple of others —Naritsune and Yasuyori—our hero, Shun Kwan, was sentenced to be marooned in the uninhabited island of Kikaigashima, situated at the south of Japan, and here they were landed in June, 1177.

But it happened that in the following year the young Empress was expecting a child, and her father Kiyomori, by way of a votive offering to the gods for her safety, determined to set free and pardon many political offenders. In pursuance of this determination, in due course a messenger came to Kikaigashima bearing a letter of pardon, but when this was opened it was found to contain but *two* names —Naritsune and Yasuyori—and neither as Shun nor Kwan was the third exile mentioned Shun Kwan was thunderstruck by this terrible discovery. "It must be a mistake," he cried, "the crime—if such it could be called—was the same, precisely the same, in each of our cases, and the punishment was also the same, why then am I only overlooked? Why, why? Let me see the letter, perhaps we have misread it, or it is wrongly written by the secretary." But no, it is perfectly clear that the letter contains no reference to him, and that looking through it again and again will not change its purport. "I must be dreaming," he said slowly at last, "wake me." Then with a miserable cry, "What shall I do alone here, when my only friends are gone? Even when we were all together the life was unsupportably lonely and oppressive, and now I am condemned to remain here quite alone." As he was lamenting thus, the messenger from Kyōto urged Naritsune and Yasuyori to get on board the boat quickly, as the day was closing in, and Shun Kwan in despair then begged the chief or captain of the sailors in charge of the boat at least to take him to an adjoining island, where there were a few inhabitants, but the unfeeling sailor would pay no attention to his appeal. Then, as the boat was actually starting, Shun Kwan attempted to climb on board, but was struck at by the sailors and compelled to loosen his hold and drop behind, still, however, imploring them to pity him and take him away. But the boat relentlessly moved away from the shore, leaving Shun Kwan a pathetic figure in the fading light. As they were going away, to freedom and happiness, the two friends called out to Shun Kwan, bidding him keep up his spirits, and promising that when they should arrive at Kyōto they would do their best to get him set free and pardoned. But neither pardon nor freedom ever came to poor Shun Kwan, and the following year, at the early age of thirty-seven, he died of exposure and privation, since nothing but sea-weed and shell fish could be found to sustain life on the desolate island of his exile. As he lay dying, a former servant, a boy who had been devoted to him, succeeded in crossing to the island from Kyōto, and did all he could to help the dying man. When death came, the boy solemnly burnt the body, and afterwards returned with the ashes, which he took and buried in Shun Kwan's native place. This rather belated and useless devotion appears to have been highly appreciated by the boy's neighbours and contemporaries

XXXII.

KIOYU AND SOFU.

(China).

As early as the 19th century B.C., the Chinese Empire already existed in the extreme eastern coast of Asia, and a much higher degree of civilisation was then enjoyed by the nation than in the majority of European countries at the same period.

In these early times the monarchy was not hereditary in one clan or family, but a suitable king was chosen in his lifetime by the reigning monarch, an arrangement which, if tradition lies not, had the happiest results, for universal peace prevailed, theft was unknown, the doors of houses were never locked, and money or a valuable accidentally dropped in the streets remained where it fell, until the owner returned to find it. This period, it is said, was marked by the last recorded appearances of the Kylin and the Hoho,* two semi-super-

*The Kylin (a name frequently misapplied to the Shishi or Lion-dog) is a composite creature something like a stag, but with one short straight horn: the Hoho is a bird somewhat resembling a large peacock, both are common objects in the art of China and Japan.

I.

II.

ONO-NO-KOMACHI.

I. From an inlaid shibuichi Tsuba in Mr. G. A. Lee's collection.

II. (From a wooden netsuke in Messrs. Yamanaka's collection.)

KIOYU & SOFU.

(From an iron Tsuba in Mr. G. A. Lee's collection.)

natural creatures, who are said only to appear on earth at times of universal peace

At the time of our story the reigning Emperor was named Gio, and, searching for his successor, his choice fell upon a learned and virtuous but rather cranky old man named Kiōyu. To him the Emperor despatched a gentleman of the court bearing an Imperial letter as well as a verbal message offering Kiōyu the reversion of the Crown. Kiōyu, however, was entirely devoted to "the simple life," and most positively declined to have anything to do with the Emperor's offer, dismissing his messenger with the scantiest courtesy possible. As soon as the latter was departed, Kiōyu went off to Yeisan waterfall to wash out of his ears the taint of the dazzling temptation to worldly honours. While he was thus engaged, it happened that his friend Sōfu, who was equally devoted to the simple life, came to the stream below the waterfall to water his ox, and catching sight of his friend performing his aural ablutions, asked him what the matter was. Kiōyu replied by telling all that had occurred, and on hearing it, Sōfu said that he could not possibly permit *his* ox to drink water that had been so horribly contaminated, and promptly led the thirsty beast away.

This little story is an exceedingly popular one in Japan, illustrating, as it is there understood, sturdy independence, and a determination to live one's own life in one's own way, unenvious of wealth, rank or power. It smacks somewhat of the incident of Alexander's interview with Diogenes.

XXXIII.

ONO-NO-KOMACHI.

(Japan, 9th Century A.D.)

At this period in Japan the making of verses was a fashionable accomplishment, and the Emperor's court contained many poets and poetesses. Of these latter Komachi was unquestionably the most celebrated, for though the details of her history are not clearly known, her poems and several dramatic novels remain to attest her abilities. She is one of "the Hundred celebrated poets," selected as such by the critics of after ages; from the hundred poets, thirty-six of special merit were again chosen, out of whom six, of superlative excellence, wear the poet's crown above their fellows, and in this last little band, Komachi is the only woman.

She is said to have been a most beautiful, charming and accomplished lady: learned in all the arts that then appertained to women of rank and refinement, and was naturally sought in marriage by many ardent suitors. To one of these, Fukakura Shosho, she promised her hand, on condition only, that he should call at her house to pay his respects to her every evening for a hundred days consecutively. This task he very cheerfully undertook, and completed up to the ninety-ninth call, when illness prevented him from keeping his final engagement, and Komachi was therefore released from hers. After this event and as the importunity of her suitors increased, she decided positively not to accept any one of them, since it was obvious that the life of the one whom she should accept would be in danger from the rejected suitors, who might not even stop short at attempting her own. And in this resolution she persevered. When she grew old she left the court, and lived entirely as a beggar, and the wizened old crone, with her dirty rags falling about her, was a living exemplification of the complexion to which the greatest beauty must come at last.

Another version of her story makes her engaged to a gentleman of the Court, named Koreaki, who was false to her and married another girl whose father was of very high rank in the Court. After this desertion, she determined never to marry, and as above related kept to her determination. This version is that most generally accepted as the truth.

And yet another story declared that she was exceedingly vain of her great beauty and wit, and expected every man as a matter of course to fall in love with her. With this disposition, she found none of her suitors good enough for her, waiting until the Shogun, or at least an Imperial Prince should propose for her hand, and as this event did not occur, she was at last left lamenting, " in maiden meditation fancy free." A Japanese writer, however, suggests that this version was probably invented by some father or mother anxious to impress on a daughter not to be too proud of her beauty or wit, but to be content with the goods the gods might send to her: marry

SHUN KWAN.

(From an ivory netsuke in Messrs. Yamanaka's collection.)

SOGA GORO & ASAHINA SABURO.

(From an ivory netsuke in Mr. H. S. Trower's collection.)

a respectable young man of her own rank, and not, in brief, cry for the moon.

Of Komachi's beauty, however, nobody had two opinions. She and Sotoori-hime, the wife of the Emperor Inkio (412-454 A.D.) are celebrated as the two most beautiful women of Japan. "She is as lovely as Komachi" is the highest expression of admiration, even at the present day.

From hundreds of her poems the following —written when she was no longer young—is selected It refers to the flowers as a symbol of beauty:—

"While I was revelling
In the thought of my beauty,
The bloom of my youth
Has faded away."

Both as a single figure, as in our illustrations, and in groups with her companion poets, Komachi appears over and over again in Japanese art: on pouch mounts, brush cases, ink pots, and writing boxes, she is a special favourite, as well as on sword furniture and other metal work.

(The first illustration from a sword-guard by Hamano Chokuzui (18th century) shows Komachi in her trailing court dress, standing beneath a cherry tree in full bloom, which is regarded in Japan as the incarnation of loveliness. the other two from netsukes, show her as an old, old woman, dressed in rags and, in one example, seated on a log of wood.)

SOME RANDOM NOTES.

⁂ The designs on the cover are by Mr. Rioko Kado, the Japanese writing literally translated is "Tales of Treasures;" the device on the back of the cover—a three-legged crow—represents the Sun, the Badge of Japan

SHAKUDO.—Bronze, with surface or patina of dark purple, sometimes almost black. It contains from 5 to 10% of gold.

SHIBUICHI.—Bronze, with surface or patina of silver grey. It contains from 25 to—in the best quality—70% of silver.

SAKE.—A liquor of the nature of beer, brewed from rice, yeast and water. It is generally heated before being drunk.

KYŌTO.—The seat of the Mikado's government from 794 to 1869 A.D.

KAMAKURA.—Near Yedo, was the seat of the Shogun's military government from 1192 to 1332 A.D. Once a great city, it is now a mere collection of half deserted temples.

KAGO.—A sedan chair, slung on a single pole, and carried on the shoulders

HONO.—The designation of a retired Emperor who had assumed a religious name.

BUSHIDO—The warlike spirit Chivalry.

SHOGUN.—Abbreviated from "Seiitai shogun," the title first given to the general who in ancient times was appointed to subjugate Ezo or northern Japan. From the time of Yoritomo, who was the first Shogun who had the power of absolutely governing, not only Ezo, but the whole of Japan, to the end of the Tokugawa Shoguns in 1867 A D., the title Shogun was of the nature rather of an honourable prefix. The last Shogun, Tokugawa Keiki, surrendered his powers into the present Emperor's hands, and retired into private life.

DAIMIO.—A feudal chief of Japan, holding his office direct from the Shogun. In 1862 there were 266 of these Daimios, who by 1869, when the entire feudal system was ended, had ceased as such to exist, both office and title then becoming extinct.

SAMURAI.—The general name for a person who was allowed, in feudal times, to wear two swords. The feudal system came to an end between 1867 and 1869; in 1870 an Imperial edict obliged every official to wear European dress or uniform, and thus at one stroke the entire pomp and circumstance of Mediæval Japanese life disappeared for ever. Seven years later, by another Imperial edict, which came into force on the 1st of January, 1877, the ancient privilege of wearing two swords was formally abolished; an order necessitated by the organization of a standing army upon European models. The entire nation acquiesced without an articulate murmur in these decrees, and presently the mounts and fittings of a large proportion of the discarded swords were distributed, as works of art of the finest description, over the rest of the civilized world. It is said that many of the blades are still in use, having been remounted in modern fashion and thus incorporated with the Europeanized uniforms

PRINTED BY ANDRÉ & SLEIGH, LTD., BUSHEY, HERTS.

Lightning Source UK Ltd.
Milton Keynes UK
UKHW021815201221
395986UK00007B/1696